**INSTRUMENTAL PLAY-ALONG**

AUDIO ACCESS INCLUDED

**PLAYBACK+**
Speed • Pitch • Balance • Loop

FAVORITE Disney SONGS

Audio arrangements by Peter Deneff

To access audio, visit:
**www.halleonard.com/mylibrary**

Enter Code
6516-7734-9942-7339

ISBN 978-1-70514-278-3

Visit Hal Leonard Online at
**www.halleonard.com**

Contact us:
**Hal Leonard**
7777 West Bluemound Road
Milwaukee, WI 53213
Email: info@halleonard.com

In Europe, contact:
**Hal Leonard Europe Limited**
42 Wigmore Street
Marylebone, London, W1U 2RN
Email: info@halleonardeurope.com

In Australia, contact:
**Hal Leonard Australia Pty. Ltd.**
4 Lentara Court
Cheltenham, Victoria, 3192 Australia
Email: info@halleonard.com.au

# CONTENTS

# THE BALLAD OF THE LONESOME COWBOY

from TOY STORY 4

OBOE

Music and Lyrics by
RANDY NEWMAN

rit.          a tempo

# EVERMORE
from BEAUTY AND THE BEAST

OBOE

Music by ALAN MENKEN
Lyrics by TIM RICE

# HOW DOES A MOMENT LAST FOREVER

from BEAUTY AND THE BEAST

OBOE

Music by ALAN MENKEN
Lyrics by TIM RICE

# HOW FAR I'LL GO

from MOANA

OBOE

Music and Lyrics by
LIN-MANUEL MIRANDA

# INTO THE UNKNOWN

from FROZEN 2

OBOE

Music and Lyrics by KRISTEN ANDERSON-LOPEZ
and ROBERT LOPEZ

# IT'S ALL RIGHT

featured in SOUL

OBOE

Words and Music by
CURTIS MAYFIELD

# LAVA
from LAVA

OBOE

Music and Lyrics by
JAMES FORD MURPHY

# LEAD THE WAY
## from RAYA AND THE LAST DRAGON

OBOE

Music and Lyrics by
JHENÉ AIKO

# THE PLACE WHERE LOST THINGS GO

from MARY POPPINS RETURNS

OBOE

Music by MARC SHAIMAN
Lyrics by SCOTT WITTMAN and MARC SHAIMAN

# NEVER TOO LATE

from THE LION KING 2019

OBOE

Music by ELTON JOHN
Lyrics by TIM RICE

# SPEECHLESS
from ALADDIN (2019)

OBOE

Music by ALAN MENKEN
Lyrics by BENJ PASEK
and JUSTIN PAUL

# TOUCH THE SKY

from BRAVE

OBOE

Music by ALEXANDER L. MANDEL
Lyrics by ALEXANDER L. MANDEL
and MARK ANDREWS

# TRY EVERYTHING
### from ZOOTOPIA

OBOE

Words and Music by SIA FURLER,
TOR ERIK HERMANSEN and MIKKEL ERIKSEN

# YOU'RE WELCOME

from MOANA

OBOE

Music and Lyrics by
LIN-MANUEL MIRANDA

# REMEMBER ME
## (Ernesto de la Cruz)
### from COCO

OBOE

Words and Music by KRISTEN ANDERSON-LOPEZ
and ROBERT LOPEZ